YINZER

BIBLE

PITTSBURGH N'@

IF YOU DON'T UNDERSTAND

GO BACK TO CLEVELAND!

YINZER BIBLE

FOURTH EDITION

YINZER BIBLE

TABLE OF CONTENTS

YINZER BIBLE

INTRODUCTION N'AT

PITTSBURGH; There is no other place like it in the world!!!   From its origination, PITTSBURGH has been a unique, one of a kind place. It is an amazing city full of strong traditions, diversity, a diverse family that is millions strong, great food, captivating sports and majestic scenery as we just scrape the surface. We believe that PITTSBURGH has the absolute strongest culture in the nation, and simply put, there is not a better city anywhere in the world.

If you are one of the great people that currently lives or perhaps at one time called PITTSBURGH home, then you understand that being a part of PITTSBURGH is something to

really be proud of. It is sort of like being in an elite club. If you are a guest; you too can feel like you are a part of something really special.

PITTSBURGH is more of a way of life than just a place on a map. It is a town where people come together and stay together like a family. But perhaps not your typical family.

The Yinzer Bible takes you through it all! We will discuss how we speak (PITTSBURGHESE), what we drink, eat, play, and so much more. We talk about some of the unique places and explore the soul of PITTSBURGH. It is a fun and informative book that every PITTSBURGHER should own and since writing this book, it is one that PITTSBURGH lovers from all over the country and world own. It is sort of a tangible piece of the city that we can all enjoy.

YINZER BIBLE

Whether you are just moving to the city, just visiting, lived here all of your life, used to live here, or just like the city, this is PITTSBURGH in a book.

The Yinzer Bible provides you with the opportunity to explore all of the wonder, fun, energy, and character of PITTSBURGH and even will give you some new ideas of things you can do in the city. We love our town and you will enjoy connecting to PITTSBURGH through this book.

CULTURE

The PITTSBURGH culture is best summed up as "Diverse". Over hundreds of years, we have had many immigrants from across the world that have established a home in the city. Many others have come to PITTSBURGH for education, employment, or many other reasons. With so many people from so many different backgrounds, there is no doubt that it is a well-diversified melting pot.

From an entertainment perspective, a good deal of the PITTSBURGH culture is centered around our three always popular professional sports teams. The PITTSBURGH Steelers, PITTSBURGH Penguins, and PITTSBURGH Pirates

are the major league teams that generate an almost religious like following in the "BURGH". Sports are a frequent conversation topic that drives energetic and passionate discussions and keeps many people enamored with the city (N'At).

Sports are more of a passion and obsession in PITTSBURGH than in most other cities. People truly rally around the teams in good times and in bad. PITTSBURGHERS really feel a strong connection to these beloved teams and our enthusiasm is unmistakable.

It is best described as a sense of being a part of something really special. PITTSBURGH sports create a family atmosphere and a common ground among all that reside in the city and well beyond. In fact, many of the friends

of the Yinzer Bible facebook page don't necessarily live in the city or even state or country.

In fact, if our local teams win, you will frequently find that people are in a better mood the next day. While I haven't done an official scientific study on this finding, it is evident from observation. And we won't even talk about what happens to the moods in PITTSBURGH if we lose.

With three championship teams that retain remarkable histories, PITTSBURGH loves its sports and has every reason to be proud.

Another part of the PITTSBURGH culture is centered around the unique and delicious food that is offered throughout the region. PITTSBURGH is a city full of so many wonderful restaurants that range in tastes, styles, ethnicities,

culture, crowds, and price points. From simple dining like those restaurants found in the university areas, to the fancy dining of downtown and Mt. Washington. Food is a part of the PITTSBURGH culture. In fact, many people center their family, social or even business interactions around a meal at one of these many restaurants.

We will talk more about food and some good choices later on in our journey.

There is no doubt that food and sports makes PITTSBURGH different. However, it is not just these two components that differentiate us. Instead, PITTSBURGH is different in many ways because of the people, traditions, and even the way we speak. Yes, we are a part of the United States and while many states blend Spanish into their culture,

we have our very own language called PITTSBURGHese

(Pronounced PITTSBURGH-eze).

PITTSBURGHESE

HOW PITTSBURGH PEOPLE SPEAK

People from out of town may be shocked to learn that there is another language besides English that is spoken in PITTSBURGH (And no, it is not Spanish).

PITTSBURGH has its own partial and unique dialect that is derived from years of evolving culture and dialects. This language is affectionately named "PITTSBURGHESE" and takes the shape of words that are spoken regularly around town by those who are likely more local to PITTSBURGH. As an evolution of varying cultures, it is this language that is one

of the unique characteristics that define the culture of PITTSBURGH today.

I must warn you though, while this way of speaking is common and widely accepted in the greater PITTSBURGH area, you will probably be looked at funny if you use it in other areas of the country.

For instance, a sentence like: "Yinz goin' dahn-tahn for sum primanti's n'at?" is a question that you very well may hear in one form or another. Translated into boring English; this question is asking if another person plans on going into the downtown area of PITTSBURGH for a Primanti's sandwich and some other accompaniments, like a beer.

This may sound strange if you don't live in the BURGH, but this is the way many of the PITTSBURGH locals

communicate and it is just one of the things that makes the city unique. It is sort of the dialect of those that understand and have lived in the city for years or quite possibly all of their life.

PITTSBURGHESE or PITTSBURGH English is the official dialect of the Yinzers. If you are in PITTSBURGH, you will hear it. Thus, if you aren't fluent in this language, what follows is a useful translator to help you communicate around "Tahn".

Now don't get scared away; Some of my fan mail asked if they could get around in plain English and the answer is of course. However, this is just part of our culture that makes it more interesting but don't fret; we all speak Boring English also.

PITTSBURGHESE DICTIONARY N'at

"*PITTSBURGHESE*"	**DEFINITION**
Ahr	Time; Hour in the day
Arhn	Iron City Beer: Iron or Iron City Beer
Babushka	Headscarf frequently worn by elderly women
Baffroom	Restroom
Burgh	Shorted version of PITTSBURGH (don't forget the "h" at the end
Bess Buys	Best Buy Store
Bear	Beer

YINZER BIBLE

Birfday	Birthday
Blinkers	Vehicle Turn Signals
Brights	Vehicle High Beams
Caawch	Couch
Cawhty	County
Selrr	Cellar / Basement
Clicker	TV Remote control
Coal	Cool
Crick	Creek
Crud	Dirt
Dahn-Tahn	Downtown PITTSBURGH

YINZER BIBLE

Dare	There
Ding	Dent on a vehicle
Doe-nit	Donut
Drawling	Drawing
Eye-Owl	Aisle
Fahr	Fire
Fillings	Feelings
Ghetto Sleigh	Pat Bus
Grahj	Garage
Greezy	Greasy
Gumband	Rubber band

Hanky	Handkerchief
Hogie	Submarine sandwich
Haus	House or Stadium
Hun	Honey
Igl	Eagle (Short for Giant Eagle)
Ignurunt	Ignorant or Rude
Jagoff	A person who is fooling around or is considered to be a jerk
Jaggin'	Teasing
Jell	Jail
Jumbo	Bologna Lunch Meat

YINZER BIBLE

Keller	Color
Kranz	Crayons
Lind	Lend / Borrow
Mawhntins	Mountains
Mum	Mom
N'At	"And That" or another way of saying And Other Things.
Nakin	Napkin
Neb	To be budding your way into another persons affairs
Pahnd	Pound

Pahr	Power
Pitcher	Picture
Pisketti	Spaghetti
Picknick	Picnic
Pop	Soda
Progee	Pierogi
Q-Pon	Coupon
Rad-ator	Radiator
Rilly	Really
Stick	Ruler
Sweeper	Vacuum cleaner

YINZER BIBLE

Red-up	To get ready
Ruff	Roof
Samitch	Sandwich
Slippy	Slippery
Stillers	A common way of saying the PITTSBURGH Steelers (Football team)
Stoop	Porch
Sumpin	Something
Tahl	Towel
Tahn	Town
Tourlet	Toilet

YINZER BIBLE

Warsh	Wash
Umbella	Umbrella
Yinz	Much like the Y'all of the South. Means a group of people to whom the speaker is referring.
Yinzer	The beloved PITTSBURGHer who speaks PITTSBURGHese and follows the culture

SPORTS

Sports are something that are played in other cities but it is more of a way of life in PITTSBURGH. The dreams begin early at the many grade school football fields across Western Pennsylvania. The kids imagine themselves suiting up in Steelers gear for an NFL game at Heinz Field. They all share the dream of one day becoming a PITTSBURGH Steeler as they discuss sports, games, players, etc.

When it comes to sports trivia and knowledge; Don't count out a young boy or girl in the PITTSBURGH area. They

are frequently as well versed in sports or even greater than many adults who follow PITTSBURGH sports.

Sports, and specifically Steeler football, are very much a year round conversation in PITTSBURGH. The Steelers have one of the largest and most loyal fan bases of any NFL team. On my Yinzer Bible page, I see football comments from my friends every single day of the year.

And the people of PITTSBURGH love the teams won't miss a game despite horrific weather conditions, sickness, or any other reason. If there is a family emergency or something urgent that must be taken care of, it can wait until after the game many would argue. It is also important not to disturb on of our die hard fans during the game as game time is much like going to a very important meeting and requires the utmost focus.

As those know who have attended a game, going to any PITTSBURGH game is fun but going to a Steelers game is an unforgettable experience that simply cannot be duplicated.

There is an enormous buzz in the city that intensifies throughout the week and percolates on game day. An excitement that everyone feels throughout the city and this feeling only intensifies as you get closer to the stadiums for some tailgating and the much anticipated kick-off.

On game day, as you make your way toward the infamous Heinz Field, you begin to notice the noise and energy of the massive crowds and are quickly engulfed in a sea of black and gold. It starts to get louder and the smell of wonderful food permeates the air as people elevate tailgating to a whole new level.

YINZER BIBLE

People are happy, excited, and having a great time anticipating the game. There are black and yellow cars, pick-up trucks, and full size RV's with people yelling, drinking their favorite beverage, laughing, and waving their Terrible Towels. It is simply pure excitement.

The food at the tailgates is nothing short of amazing. Forget simple hamburgers and hotdogs (that still hold spots on some of the BBQ's); many people in PITTSBURGH are frying wings, grilling Kielbasa, roasting pigs, or even eating crab legs and lobster tails (typically sourced from Wholey's in the strip of course).

Quiet is not a word that would describe this experience. The Steelers chants can be heard from miles away including the famous PITTSBURGH Super Bowl song that we typically start singing in pre-season (with utmost confidence).

As game time approaches, the parking lots empty as people flood into the stadiums with their game faces on and minds on the game (and some of the traditional stadium foods). Once in the stadium, the attitude quickly changes from partying to down to business. Aggression towards the rivals is prevalent as the stadium fills with an absolute hatred for the other team. Fueling the hatred is a hops and barley brew that is downed in massive quantities.

A low rumbling growl seems to be ever present in the stadiums and it erupts into a deafening roar as plays unfold. As the Steelers inevitably score, the entire stadium shakes and you can't help but feel chills that will be sent up and down your spine. It is a feeling that is really indescribable.

Speaking of chills, the temperatures and conditions don't really matter in Steeler country. Steeler fans are

absolutely committed to the game and the worse the conditions, the louder they get.

PITTSBURGH is used to inclement weather in PITTSBURGH and we dress for the occasion. In the worst conditions, be sure to look for our handful of shirtless fans sporting huge beer bellies with stretched Steelers messaging. They are a hoot.

People in PITTSBURGH take football very seriously. In fact, this was never more obvious than when the previous Steelers stadium (called Three Rivers Stadium) was torn down to make room for the new stadium. Steelers fans were in full attendance for this event. The entire night before the demolition, people were tailgating, cheering, and some, even crying.

Steeler football is actually lived in PITTSBURGH (and beyond by its fans). If you haven't recently experienced a game, it is something to put on your priority list as there are very few experiences like this anywhere in the world.

With this said, football is not the only game in town. Baseball is also a sport that PITTSBURGH truly enjoys. In fact, PITTSBURGH has had a long love affair with baseball. In 1903, PITTSBURGH played in the first World Series and have had some terrific seasons over the years with several pennants and world series under its belt.

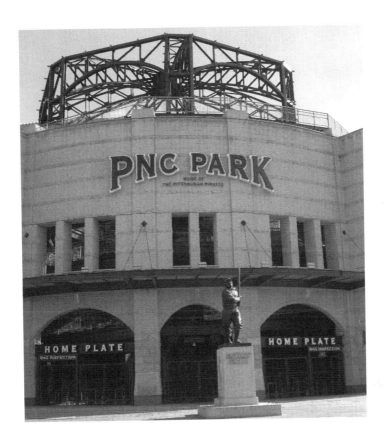

The PITTSBURGH Pirates (sometimes called the "Bucs") have an absolutely beautiful ballpark for spending some time watching our team in action. Many have voted this

modern stadium to be one of the very best in the league due to amenities, view, and so much more.

The Pirates game experience is much more tame than the Steeler experience and is an excellent family activity. The team is always fun to watch and there is plenty of good food at the stadium.

The grass is always perfectly manicured on the field, the seats are comfortable, and I am not sure there is a bad seat in the house. Even the position of the stadium is angled so you can take in the view of downtown PITTSBURGH.

The Buc's have seen up and down seasons but there is something that is quintessentially nostalgic about taking in a baseball game at our wonderful field. It really brings many back to time spent at the ballpark with their family.

YINZER BIBLE

The Penguins complete our sports trio. It seems like year after year, the Penguins (or "Pens" or "Guins") always seem to give the league a run for its money with some amazing talent.

The talent over the years has allowed the team to win several Stanley Cups and have produced some remarkable Hall of Fame talent including the legendary Mario Lemieux.

Going to a Pens game is another must do activity. The fans really get behind the team and our beloved Pens always have a lot of heart to support their talent.

It seems like you can hear the Lets Go Pens chant from the other side of the city when the team is playing along with the prominent hits of the PITTSBURGH defensemen.

The new arena (that replaced the aging Civic Arena) seems to deliver even a more exciting performance that was only once enjoyed at the former arena called "The Igloo".

So whether it is hockey, baseball, or football, PITTSBURGH sports are a great part of our city that is enjoyed by people from across the nation.

TERRIBLE TOWEL

The terrible Towel is the quintessential Steelers and PITTSBURGH sports cheering device. It was developed around 1975 by a famous PITTSBURGH broadcaster named Myron Cope who wanted to bring something unique to PITTSBURGH fans.

It is a simple yellow hand towel with black writing that is powerful in its meaning. It is used to rally the local team and inflame the crowds. It is also believed to distract and weaken our opponents. We wave it proud and high at all sporting events!

YINZER BIBLE

At any PITTSBURGH game you can see thousands of these towels spinning in the stands. Some even say that the wind chills increase by five miles per hour after a touchdown as these mini cotton turbines spin up PITTSBURGH in all its glory.

They are a wonderful accessory to our PITTSBURGH fashion that all points to our love for PITTSBURGH sports.

YINZER STYLE

PITTSBURGHERS have always been more eccentric with their hair styles. The true Yinzer crowd represents us the best with hair styles that make the heads turn.

For women, the frizzy hair and big bangs create the hair style that makes its mark and never gets old. The bangs should have enough hair spray in them to withstand forty-mile hour gusts in a stadium but should not be so tall that they disrupt the view of the spectators behind.

YINZER BIBLE

Make-up needs to be applied very generously for women. Whenever a Yinzer puts on lipstick, the rule is to put on a little too much, and then put on much, much more. As a general rule of thumb, your lips should be as bright as a traffic light.

For men, it is a bit more complicated. The preferred hair cut is the mullet. The mullet is more of a work of art than just a haircut and it is not mistakable. This is not your typical barbershop kind of haircut.

The key to the mullet is to have it long on the top and very short on the sides. The back should be curly but can also be straight. However, it should cover the neck to the shoulders.

YINZER BIBLE

The mullet is more than a haircut, it is a symbol of true devotion to PITTSBURGH. The people wearing the traditional mullets in PITTSBURGH are truly the kings among men.

For both men and women, tight stone washed jeans are always in style in Yinzer fashion and rock like DVE. They should be just one size too short and should be accompanied by beat up white tennis shoes.

When it comes to wardrobe colors, there is no question. PITTSBURGH bleeds black and gold. We absolutely love these two beautiful colors together and it is found absolutely everywhere; from bridges, to buildings, to food, clothing, signs, etc. We sport our team colors everywhere.

> Quick Fact: Wiz might say Black N Yellow in his song but we are truly Black & Gold!!

In fact, if you open up any true PITTSBURGHERS closet, you will find these two colors to comprise most of their wardrobe as well as their bedding, wall decorations, floor mats, cups, signs, and much more. The colors go with everything and should be worn everywhere.

We also refuse to throw away any Black and Gold memorabilia as it is considered sacrilegious and even bad

luck. In fact, if you look closely around town, you will find old PITTSBURGH championship shirts with print so faded that you can barely read it. These old battered historical testaments are great apparel for tailgates or a night on the town. In fact, one of my favorite jerseys belongs to Jerome Bettis, AKA "The Bus" (former Steeler running back). Old or new, we just want you to represent the PITTSBURGH teams!

THE SECRETS OF PITTSBURGH

PITTSBURGH is full of secrets and interesting history. Many of the people in PITTSBURGH can tell you stories about before a building was constructed, or what it was like in a particular area in a particular ere. There are just so many to share but a few of the lesser known secrets that are sort of fun to know.

What is interesting about these old facts about PGH is that even many natives of PITTSBURGH do not know about them. Thus, if you are a native or visitor, these interesting facts are a good find that you can share with others.

Gulf Tower

YINZER BIBLE

The Gulf Building is a 44 story building that was built in 1932. Besides being a core office building for many companies, for many years, the Gulf Tower was also known as the weatherman of PITTSBURGH.

The top stepped section of the building would notify PITTSBURGH residents, those who could see the building, of the forecast. It accomplished this through a series of neon colors that illuminated this upper portion of the building. The color changed depending on the weather conditions and could be seen from miles away because of the height of the building.

This was long before iPhones and the internet so although it was quite a rudimentary system, it was a useful system. Flashing blue meant cold with precipitation, constant blue meant fair and colder; constant orange meant warmer and fair; flashing orange meant warmer with precipitation.

More recently, however, just the glass panels at the very top of the building provide the forecasting and it is a bit more limited. The glass glows blue for precipitation and red for fair weather.

People used to wonder how the building knew to change colors. How could it tell the forecast and how did it automatically switch to the appropriate color. It was actually much simpler than that. It was an employee of the building that was to make the switch with simple controls located within the building.

Grant Building

YINZER BIBLE

The 37 floor Grant Building located on the South side of the city was constructed in 1930 and was one of the earlier skyscrapers in the City of PITTSBURGH.

For many years, the building boasted a very large antenna at the top of the structure. This antenna, believed to have risen 150 additional feet, was illuminated. Every night the antenna (that also served as an aviation beacon) would flash "P-I-T-T-S-B-U-R-G-H" in morse code. People have said that this messaging could be seen from as far as 150 miles away.

Today a smaller antenna sits on top of the building but still with the same purpose and still with the same message (for those that know the code).

PITTSBURGH Clock

The large 35 foot tall and 226 foot wide clock sitting midway up the steep hill of Mt. Washington was erected in the 1920's. This sign has prominent red lettering that has been a clock and billboard in the city for many years.

It was placed on the Mount Washington hillside near the Duquesne Incline tracks. Its earliest known advertisers were Iron City Beer, Clark's Teaberry Gum and WTAE-TV Channel 4. In 1967, the Alcoa aluminum company took over the sign and changed its plain background into a gray-and-white mosaic font pattern that spelled out PITTSBURGH when seen in the daytime, giving the sign new popularity. Alcoa became

the sign's most well-known advertiser, remaining for the next 25 years. In 1992, Miles Laboratories moved their U.S. headquarters from Elkhart, Indiana to PITTSBURGH and became the sign's new advertiser. In April 1995, the Miles brand name was absorbed by its parent company, Bayer AG. Since then, the sign has featured the Bayer name and its circular cross logo.

One of the more interesting parts of the sign is something not so obvious. If you look closely, you will see the word "P-I-T-T-S-B-U-R-G-H," written in the gray and white background. This can really only be made out during the day and it is a bit hard to decipher even on a good day.

The sign is capable of providing more than just a company or advertisement; As pictured is a welcome

message during a G20 Summit that was held in PITTSBURGH.

INCLINES

PITTSBURGH features two inclines called the Duquesne Incline and Monongahela Incline. Since the 1870's,

these inclines have been carrying passengers up and down the PITTSBURGH mountainside via a steep vertical track.

The Duquesne Incline like its sister is an inclined plane railroad. It is towers above PITTSBURGH's infamous South Side neighborhood and scaling Mt. Washington. Designed by Samuel Diescher, the incline was completed in 1877 and is 800 feet (244 m) long, 400 feet (122 m) in height, and is inclined at a 30 degree angle. It is an unusual track gauge of 5 ft (1,524 mm).

Originally steam powered, the Duquesne Incline was built to carry cargo up and down Mt. Washington in the late 19th century. It later carried passengers, particularly Mt. Washington residents who were tired of walking up footpaths to the top. Inclines were then being built all over Mt. Washington. But as more roads were built on "Coal Hill" most

of the other inclines were closed. By the end of the 1960s, only the sister Monongahela Incline and the Duquesne Incline remained.

In 1962, the Duquesne incline was closed, apparently for good. Major repairs were needed, and with so few patrons, the incline's private owners did little. But local Duquesne Heights residents launched a fund-raiser to help the incline. It was a tremendous success, and on July 1, 1963, the incline reopened under the backings of a non-profit organization dedicated to its preservation. Pittsburgh will always be grateful.

The incline has since been totally refurbished. The cars, have been stripped of paint to reveal the original wood. An observation deck was added at the top affording a magnificent view of PITTSBURGH's "Golden Triangle".

The inclines are driven by an engine that is located in the upper station. The cars always move in synch as they are counterbalanced to one another. As one car descends, it pulls up the other car. Thus, the motor only needs to generate enough power to overcome some of the friction and the varying weight of the passengers on either incline.

The inclines are now one of the city's most popular tourist attractions. PITTSBURGH is very much defined by these unique cars that provide some of the most unforgettable views in the city as well as a ride through history.

The Duquesne incline is located on the side of Mt. Washington. It neighbors some of the more fancy dining (including Monterey Bay, Georgetown Inn, Isabella's, Tin Angel, LeMont, etc).

The Monongahela incline is closer to the many overlooks on Mt. Washington. When off boarding at the bottom of the Monongahela incline, you will find that you are

within steps of Station Square. No matter which you choose,
you are in for a wonderful experience that is as fun for those of
9 months to 90 years of age and beyond.

PITTSBURGH VS. PITTSBURG

PITTSBURGH is even spelled more uniquely than other Burg's. Most Burg's (Harrisburg, Plattsburg, etc.) do not have an "H" at the end of the name but PITTSBURGH most certainly does.

One interesting historical fact is that PITTSBURGH temporarily lost its "H" in 1891. However, people petitioned and demand the letter back. The people won and PITTSBURGH was re-granted the "H" several decades later by the U.S. Board of Geographic Names.

YINZER BIBLE

It is clear that we covet every letter of our sacred town and we will fight for every one of them. I think that the simple "H" stands for **History** and this History is a coveted part of this proud city. It is not simply a place on a map but instead a historical American city that boast so many unique chapters of American history that spans generations and generations.

This sort of history simply cannot be replicated. A place either has it or it doesn't but PITTSBURGH has it in spades!

PITTSBURGH EATS

Eclectic Food

Who doesn't love a great meal; Well in PITTSBURGH you will find countless wonderful dining experiences that will make sure your taste buds leave entirely satisfied.

PITTSBURGH is the quintessential model of the melting pot. Within the area you find the descendants of many countries and cultures. In fact, because the city is so old, there are now several generations of families from these various cultures that have grown up in PITTSBURGH but carry on their proud traditions from where they originated.

YINZER BIBLE

For example, you can look to Bloomfield as the Little Italy of PITTSBURGH. Germans tend to reside on Troy Hill and the North Side. The Jewish culture is strong in Squirrel Hill. And the list goes on and on.

It only makes sense that if you want the good authentic grub, these are the places that you will want to head.

The food in these areas is taken very seriously and you can easily find yourself in a restaurant with great ethnically accurate food, interesting drinks, and diverse people.

Food is important to the city and there are many restaurants in PITTSBURGH. It would be impossible to name them all so let's look at some highlights and favorites of the city.

Primanti Brothers (PITTSBURGH's Sandwich)

Original Location: Strip District: 46 18th Street,

PITTSBURGH, PA 15222, Phone: (412) 263-2142

Food is a subject that PITTSBURGH takes very seriously and if you could identify a sandwich that defines the

city, it would unquestionably be the oversized Primanti's sandwich.

The idea of a massive sandwich with fries and coleslaw on the sandwich may sound repulsive to some out-of-towners, but in PITTSBURGH, this is what we eat and believe me, it works very well. So much so, that there is now a mailing service for those throughout the country that cannot enjoy this wonderful creation.

These sandwiches have been famous for decades and are the perfect choice for a late night snack after a night of fun at the bars, a good lunch break stop, perfect stadium food, or really just about any time. In fact, the Strip District (the original location) is cranking out these sandwiches 24 hours a day.

YINZER BIBLE

You may ask yourself; Who is pulling up a stool at 3:00 AM at Primanti's? Well the list is long. You will be rubbing elbows next to many intoxicated bar goers, the truck drivers that supply the strip district, college students, and many night shift emergency personnel to name a few.

There aren't many rules at Primanti's but the only major guideline to follow is to get the sandwich as it comes. Asking for fries and "slaw" on the side is frowned upon and gives you away as an out of towner. I know that it might not sound good together but it is amazing!

When it comes to food in PITTSBURGH, there is no better way to taste the city than to enjoy our signature sandwich. Sink your teeth (and most of your face) into a delicious primanti's sandwich with a cold Iron City to wash it down and you know you are home.

YINZER BIBLE

Besides being an institution in PITTSBURGH, this is also a place for love to develop. In PITTSBURGH, taking a first date to Primanti's is perfectly acceptable. In fact, it is an exercise of acceptance. If you can watch your date scarf a sloppy sandwich down, while getting it all over their face, and you still feel the same way about them afterward; well then you (Yinz) guys very well may be in love.

Pierogis Plus (Pierogis)

342 Island Avenue, McKees Rocks, PA 15136, Phone: (412) 331-2224

With the influence of Eastern Europe in PITTSBURGH, Pierogis are a staple of the Yinzer diet. This potato, onion,

and cheese stuffed masterpiece is what PITTSBURGH runs on and is a must do for anyone that hasn't tried one.

There are many varieties of Pierogis to try but there is no better place to try it then Pierogis Plus.

It is worth noting that Pierogis Plus is not a white napkin, dine in kind of a place. It is a converted gas station that has a little door where you order and then take it with you. You can get them frozen, hot, or cold but these little delicacies always hit the spot and are a favorite of the locals.

It is an interesting place to see. It may not be at the top of the tourism list but at some point, you need to find your way over to this joint and give it a try.

The Original Hot Dog (Fries & Hot Dogs)

3901 Forbes Ave, PITTSBURGH, PA Phone: (412) 621-7388

The "Original Hot Dog Shop" that PITTSBURGHERS just call the "O" is a place where french fry lovers can find their mecca. This is a restaurant that is in Oakland on the University of PITTSBURGH campus. If you are looking for atmosphere, this is probably not where you want to go but if you want amazing fries, then you just found your spot!

YINZER BIBLE

A small order of fries is very inexpensive and is absolutely enormous! It is literally a pile of fries the size of your head.

I frequently hear a couple of people from out of town debating on the size thinking that perhaps they should get a large. When they do, their eyes are large when they look at the massive stack of fries in front of them.

With fries that are double fried and cooked in peanut oil for crispiness, there is no better place to get fries in the BURGH.

The "O" also has great dogs and some other items but if you order the fries, you may find that you have little room for anything else.

Minneos Pizza House (Pizza & Hoagies)

2128 Murray Ave # 1, PITTSBURGH, PA 15217, Phone: (412) 521-9864

Minneos Pizza is a well-known pizza place in PITTSBURGH. With locations in Squirrel Hill and in the South

Hills, you won't go wrong with what is known to be some of the very best pizza in PITTSBURGH.

It is generally New York style pizza with plenty of cheese and a good crisp crust. It is unquestionably a favorite for the locals and visitors alike.

If you order peperoni and mushroom toppings on your pizza, you will frequently find it baked underneath the cheese. However, with their wonderful sicilian style thick slices, it will be on top.

They have several locations but no matter which one you find, you will love it! If you try Minneo's or my other favorite (Fiori's – South Hills), you may just say goodbye to chain pizzerias for the rest of your life!

YINZER BIBLE

Uncle Sam's (Cheesesteaks)

5808 Forbes Ave, PITTSBURGH, PA 15217, Phone: (412) 521-7827

Cheesesteaks are something that Pennsylvania is well known for and PITTSBURGH does them incredibly well. In fact, many feel that the cheesesteaks in PITTSBURGH are far better than those found in our sister city of Philadelphia (even though we are not as well known for this food).

The best of these cheesesteaks can be found at Uncle Sam's in Oakland, Squirrel Hill, or in Robinson (near the airport). They use high quality steak and have great portions. It is everything a cheesesteak should be and we will take on a Philly steak any day of the week.

We didn't sign on to the whole "Wit" or "Wiz" styles. They just make incredible cheesesteaks a more traditional way. If you go, the Ultra Uncle Sam's Special is my favorite. With extra meat, chees, onions, peppers, fresh baked bread, etc., it is very hard to beat.

Quaker Steak and Lube (Wings)

110 Andrew Drive, PITTSBURGH, PA 15275, Phone: (412) 494-3344

PITTSBURGH is well known for its love affair with wings. I have many visitors from out of town that tell me that they simply cannot get the same quality wings that we find all over our city. There are so many restaurants that offer such

great wings that you would be hard pressed to pick a best. I like wings and it is hard to pass by a place that specializes in them. Many people defer to Quaker Steak and Lube in Robinson (near the PITTSBURGH airport) as the best. They have a ton of different sauce selections and a very fun atmosphere. A good choice for the wing lovers.

It was also an establishment featured on the Food Networks *Man Versus Food*. The host of the show (Adam) took on the hottest wings the restaurant offers and found himself with a bigger battle than he anticipated.

This restaurant offers more varieties than you could imagine and any heat level that you can take. Believe me; if you like hot wings, this place will meet your "Scoville Units" (or heat level desire) perfectly. Or if you want to venture into the unknown, they can also accommodate you.

Quaker Steak and Lube is a great venue is always a good place for a showdown with some friends. Best of all, it is a great place to satisfy your wing craving.

My Big Fat Greek Gyro (Gyro)

665 WASHINGTON ROAD, MT. LEBANON, PA 15228, Phone: 412-531-4976

We like our gyro's in PITTSBURGH and the best gyro in the city is believed to belong to My Big Fat Greek Gyro located in Mt. Lebanon (South Hills) or one of its other locations. They have chicken and lamb variants with excellent portions and prices. These are great eats and a favorite of many in the city.

My Big Fat Greek Gyro has expanded to several locations now but the recipe remains the same; good portions, good value, and good eats.

One great thing about it is that you are not frowned upon if you pronounce it differently than some authentic Greek accent that pronounces it "Yeer-Oh". In PITTSBURGH, we call it Ji-Row and we don't make any apologies.

Cat on a Stick *(Kabobs)*

City chicken or "cat on a stick" is pork, chicken, veal, or a mystery meat that is cooked on a short wooden skewer. While the South Side used to have a truck on East Carson Street (South Side) that would whip up these yummy treats for

the bar goers, that food truck is now gone and the Strip District is now the best place to find this delicacy.

The name ("Cat on a Stick") came from college students that were not sure whether it was chicken or cat that they were consuming while in a bit of an alcohol dazed state of humor. Either way, they loved it. It used to be that any good bar night, you would find a line of a dozen or so intoxicated people waiting for their "cat on a stick." Patiently waiting and meowing to pass the time in line.

Today's "Cat on a Stick" patron seems to be quieter than before but we still love the food with its delicious sauce which was called "Moon Sauce". And the great things about availability in the Strip District is that you can eat one of these in the daylight. Near Wholey's in the Strip District, it is an almost impossible street food to pass by.

YINZER BIBLE

Enrico Biscotti (Biscotti)

2022 Penn Ave, PITTSBURGH, PA 15222, Phone: (412) 281-2602

A biscotti is a long, hard cookie of sorts with European roots. If you wander into Enrico Biscotti's in the Strip District, you can take a bite into one of their many, many flavors of biscotti's.

The first time you try a biscotti, you may think that you received on that was stale. However, biscotti is designed to be very hard and crunchy and a perfect chaser to a nice cat on a stick but probably more enjoyed with a cup of coffee.

YINZER BIBLE

Max's Allegheny Tavern

537 Suismon Street, PITTSBURGH, PA 15212, Phone: (412) 231-1899

A great place to find excellent German food is Max's Tavern on the North Side. The restaurant is just down the road from Allegheny General Hospital and offers some of the most authentic German food you will find in PITTSBURGH.

The restaurant features recipes and food from Germany and truly delivers for those that want authentic German food.

Historically in a German part of town, this is a restaurant that has been serving PITTSBURGH brats, sausages, and more for years and is loved by the locals.

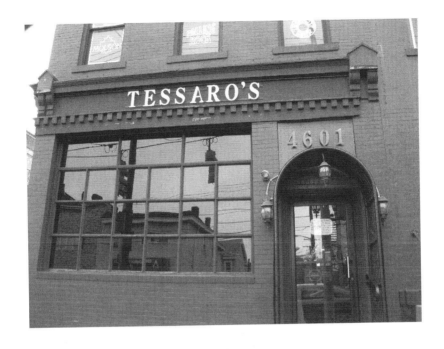

Tessaros Restaurant

4601 Liberty Ave, PITTSBURGH, Phone: (412) 682-6809

A good restaurant in the Bloomfield area is Tessaro's restaurant. It offers great burgers, steaks, and so much more.

It is a place that been a corner stone in Bloomfield and if you walk anywhere near the restaurant, the wood grill smells alone will lure you in.

On Thursday's you can find a special of Ribs which have been a crowd pleasing favorite for many years. In fact, nothing has changed in many years. The quaint feeling in the restaurant, delicious food, and wonderful smells have not changed in years. In fact, I visited this place as a child and now have a family of my own that also loves to dine at Tessaro's.

Jumbo

PITTSBURGH loves its "Jumbo". For those who aren't familiar, Jumbo is a sidewalk delicacy that most people simply

categorize as bologna lunch meat. Usually served cold and in-between two pieces of plain white bread, many kids and adults have turned to this wonderful meat to satisfy their cravings or lunch box meals.

Kielbasa

"Kielbasa" is the PITTSBURGH choice sausage (of central European decent). It is that is always a favorite at the sporting tailgates. Cooked on a charcoal or gas grill and with a bun (frequently with a yellow mustard), it is a delightful alternative to the well known hotdog. In fact, the Brats and Kielbasa are the meats that frequently fuels the roar of the PITTSBURGH crowd and excellent choices on a chilly game day (especially for the Steeler crowd).

Chipped Chopped Ham

Chipped ham is simply ham sliced and chopped in a really thin manner. It can be found at just about any PITTSBURGH grocery store and is a perfect compliment to plain white bread. This sandwich is a regular lunchtime treat for those at work.

It is interesting how this simple sandwich (or "Samwich") brings back memories to people. Many lunch boxes in PITTSBURGH frequently packed this yummy treat to our youngsters over many generations.

BRIDGES

With roughly 450 bridges in the greater PITTSBURGH area, the city is informally known as the "City of bridges". This is not that much of a stretch considering the city is in the center of three major rivers.

While many bridges are spectacular, the Three Sisters Bridges and the Smithfield Street bridges get the most attention. These bridges are not just simple jumps across the river but instead paint part of PITTSBURGH most gorgeous skyline.

The Three Sister Bridges are the three identical yellow bridges (6th, 7th, and 9th) that connect the City to the North Shore and Stadiums. They currently carry names of PITTSBURGH residents but the names do change from time

to time so I keep track of them by street number which tends to remain consistent.

The Three Sister Bridges are known to be some of the few self-anchored, self suspension bridges in the nation and are prominently painted in the BURGH'S famous yellow.

Smithfield Street Bridge

The Smithfield Street Bridge is called the "Kissing Fishes" bridge because it looks like two fishes kissing (when looking at it from certain angles). This is known to be the beginning of bridges in the PITTSBURGH area and was the first bridge river crossing into the city.

YINZER BIBLE

Now double the size and more spectacular than ever, this bridge is a awe inspiring site, especially at night when illuminated. It is now serves the main connection point between Station Square and the City of PITTSBURGH.

Bridges are part of our every day life in PITTSBURGH and we are very proud and fortunate to have such beauty surrounding these important structures.

SHOPPING

Shopping around the greater PITTSBURGH area is a shoppers dream. PITTSBURGH features all of the high-end stores you would expect in any large city including malls that rival just about any other city.

PITTSBURGH also has some extraordinarily unique places to shop. One of the most diverse and most popular is the Strip District which is a wonderfully vibrant wholesale market. Many people will tell you that the best shopping in the BURGH is found in the Strip District.

YINZER BIBLE

Strip District:

The Strip District (Frequently called "The Strip") features so many unique items that cannot be found anywhere else in the city or surrounding area. Whether it is unique PITTSBURGH memorabilia, local fresh food, flowers, toys, exotic ingredients, and even furniture, the Strip District has it all.

Not only does the Strip District have great shopping, it is an experience of its own with unique people, smells, tastes, music, and much more. It is a place where you can people watch and get a very good appreciation of the PITTSBURGH culture.

YINZER BIBLE

If you are going to spend time in the Strip District, you would be well advised to take your time. It is so easy to rush from point A to point B but in between you will miss so much. In fact, you could spend the better part of the day exploring the Strip and would absolutely taken back by all of the amazing treasures that this area of town has to offer.

It is a fast paced section of town but trust me when I tell you to slow down and take it all in. Walk through the stores and enjoy what you find as it beats any mall!

Shadyside:

If you are looking for a little bit more tame and upscale shopping, then the Shadyside area is a nice choice for a more

sophisticated day out. High-end shops and restaurants adorn Walnut Street which is the heart of Shadyside.

You can stop in for a cup of coffee at the always pleasant Coffee Tree Roasters (5524 Walnut Street, PITTSBURGH, PA 15232, 412.621.6880) and be sure to drop in next door at ToadFlax (5500 Walnut Street, PITTSBURGH, PA 15232, 412.621.2500) where you can spend hours looking at the eclectic inventory. Whether you need a gift for someone else or just something for yourself, you may find it here. Although Shadyside is not a large area, some of the restaurants, bars, and shops are some of the greatest finds.

YINZER BIBLE

Bargain Hunting and the Deals:

One of the best places to find a deal on name brands is at the Tanger Outlets (Located at *2200 Tanger Boulevard, Washington, PA 15301, Phone: (724) 225-8435*).

As you drive into the parking lot, you will see license plates from many different states. That is because people come from many states to visit the Tanger Outlets located only 25 minutes south of the city. This outlet complex offers some of the best deals around on some of the most popular stores in the country (Brooks Brothers, Sacks, Nike, Polo, Banana Republic, Carters, Adidas, Old Navy, Coach, etc.). A deal can always be found here and these savings will allow you to spend more money on other fun things that interest you in the city.

I am always shocked to find the value of these name brands and the savings may just pay for a host of other activities you choose to embrace in PITTSBURGH. In fact, one fan told me that they saved enough to buy Steeler tickets to their favorite rival game.

Mega Interesting Store:

A great mega store that is a must see is PITTSBURGH's IKEA store located in the Robinson area. This unique and massive home store has just about anything you can use, attach, or put into a home, apartment, or dorm room. And the best part is that most everything in the store is very inexpensive.

YINZER BIBLE

If you go there just before the university semester starts, you will find hundreds upon hundreds of students obtaining what they need to get their dorms and apartments ready for the semester.

IKEA is a Swedish brand and only has a select number of stores. When you find yourself near one, visit one!

Alternate Shopping:

The Waterfront: The Waterfront is a redeveloped area located in Homestead (149 W. Bridge Street, Homestead, PA 15120). It is an outdoor shopping area with roughly 70 shops, restaurants, and a movie theatre. It includes the usual suspects for any suburban shopping area but is located closer to the city.

Traditional Mall:

If you are looking for a great mall, the best mall in PITTSBURGH is Ross Park Mall in the North Hills. *(1000 Ross Park Mall Drive, PITTSBURGH, PA 15237, Phone: 412.369.4401).* It is a huge mall that has some very unique stores and great restaurants. It is a good choice for the more traditional shopping experience.

Ross Park also offers some very high-end stores including Louis Vuitton, Burberry, Coach, Kate Spade, etc. Flanking each other you will also find LL Bean and the Cheesecake Factory that are two of my favorites for shopping and dining.

THE QUICK FACTS OF PITTSBURGH

So let's talk about some of the stats. PITTSBURGH is the second-largest city in Pennsylvania (just behind Philadelphia) and is nationally ranked 22nd in the U.S.[1]

The population of the city is only a few hundred thousand but increased to over two million if you include the greater PITTSBURGH area (outside of downtown) where many suburbs reside.

YINZER BIBLE

The city features over roughly 150 high rise buildings and approximately 450 bridges in the City (closer to 1800 if you count the surrounding area).

PITTSBURGH was once known as the "City of Bridges" and rivals only Venice, Italy in the total number of bridges (although some stats suggest that PGH outnumbers Venice).

As many people know, the city was once legendary for its place in history as a steel town. However, today steel production is little to almost non-existent and the economy is driven by healthcare, energy, technology, education, fuel, and financial services.

CLIMATE

PITTSBURGH features all four seasons and does so with beauty. In fact, the four seasons are one of my favorite aspects of the city as you get a true representation of every season.

Winter (Football and Hockey Season) can be chilly (averaging in the upper 20's° F) and you should count on snow from December through March. While many from the southern states despise snow, it helps makes the holiday season much more fun and is also good for the winter activities such as gazing at the massive Christmas displays at

Hartwood Acres and Oglebay, skiing at Hidden Valley or Seven Springs, or just some ice skating downtown (Dahn-Tahn).

Summers (Baseball season) are warm with temperatures averaging in the upper 70's to mid 80's°F. Summer boasts so many fun activities and is a great time to visit the Burgh if you are from out of town.

Spring is simply grand. Climbing out from a cold winter, Spring greets us with amazing flowers and colors that are sprinkled across the city. The flowers in the Spring are truly breathtaking.

Fall (Football Season - Steelers) marks a time for unmatched beauty. Western, PA is painted with vibrant colors

and crisp cool air. The fall foliage is unforgettable and you will feel the buzz of the PITTSBURGH Steelers.

The city is beautiful any time a year but these seasons help make this city as picturesque as you can find. There is simply not a bad time of year in PITTSBURGH if you embrace all that the city has to offer.

ARTS AND CULTURE

ENTERTAINMENT

There is another side to the city that is quite opposite of its very well-known and well-respected sporting side. PITTSBURGH is very wealthy in the arts and culture thanks to many non-profit organizations and the donations of many wealthy residents (both past and present).

PITTSBURGH museums are plentiful and include the PITTSBURGH Center for the Arts, the Andy Warhol Museum,

the Carnegie Museum of Art, the Frick Art & Historical Center, and the Carnegie Science Center among others. You guessed it; some of these names are some of the wealthiest names in history that provided major funding and grants for the PITTSBURGH culture long after they were gone.

PITTSBURGH features The Cultural District located in downtown (Dahn-Tahn) where the classic arts can be appreciated. The Benedum Center, The Byham Theater, The O'Reilly Theater, Allegheny Riverfront Park are just a few of our venues that hold shows. The PITTSBURGH Symphony Orchestra performs in the ever-majestic Heinz Hall complex, and the PITTSBURGH Opera performs in the gorgeous Benedum Center. We also have the PITTSBURGH Dance Council and the PITTSBURGH Ballet Theater that hold

various dance events. There are also countless other galleries and museums.

It is truly a well-rounded and diverse city that has much to offer in arts and entertainment to appreciate.

VISITING: WHERE TO STAY

If you are staying in PITTSBURGH for the first time, you may not be sure of the best place to stay. There are many great hotels in the area but if you really want to experience the city, the best advice is to stay downtown where

much of the action can be found (or at least you will be centrally located).

Two of the best hotels in downtown are the historic Omni William Penn and the modern Fairmont.

Omni William Penn

*530 William Penn Place, PITTSBURGH, Pennsylvania 15219
(Phone: 412.281.7100)*

The Omni is a historic hotel located close to the arena and Strip District. It is an older hotel with rich history and is centrally located on Grant Street (front of building).

This hotel is a great place to stay if you want a traditional older hotel in downtown PITTSBURGH. The lobby is nothing short of grand and boast marble, and cathedral ceilings.

Built from 1915 to 1916, the $6 million William Penn opened on March 11, 1916, in what newspapers hailed as the Grandest Hotel in the nation, its first night it hosted the annual PITTSBURGH Chamber of Commerce Gala and was

recorded as the largest gala in city history up to that time with U.S. Secretary of State Philander Knox hosting the event. The original hotel covered the western half of the block, facing Mellon Square.

The Omni William Penn Hotel is a twenty three floor (3 underground) hotel located at 530 William Penn Place on Mellon Square in downtown. A variety of luminaries have stayed at the hotel, including John F. Kennedy. The hotel has won numerous awards including being named one of the best for weddings.

Omni William Penn Hotel, PITTSBURGH is a member of Historic Hotels of America, the official program of the National Trust for Historic Preservation.

The hotel also features an award winning restaurant that dates from 1916, the Terrace Room, featuring among other amenities a wall long mural entitled "The taking of Fort Pitt". However, you would probably be well-advised to try many of the other restaurants in Pittsburgh first.

Fairmont

510 Market Street, PITTSBURGH, Pennsylvania 1522

(Phone: 412.773.8800)

Alternatively the Fairmont is located in the center of town closer to the stadiums and Market Square.

The Fairmont is an upscale hotel with the most central location in the city for attractions, restaurants, and sporting events. It is a luxurious hotel of over 150 rooms and features the latest high-end amenities.

The Sheraton in Station Square *(300 W Station Square Dr, PITTSBURGH, Pennsylvania 15219, Phone: (412) 261-2000)* is yet another option with a very nice view of the city and of course the heavenly bed.

The Sheraton is located just across the river from PITTSBURGH and recently underwent a large renovation.

Another enticing option is the Courtyard PITTSBURGH Downtown (945 Penn Ave, PITTSBURGH, PA 15222, Phone:

(412) 434-5551) which along with the Westin, are close to the Convention Center and Strip District.

There are also a few options that are adjacent to the stadiums that may be a little less costly but lack the convenience of the other areas.

The end result, as long as you are staying in PITTSBURGH, you are off to a great start as this city is very walkable.

WHERE WE PLAY

STADIUMS & ARENA

The two professional sports stadiums in PITTSBURGH are named Heinz Field and PNC Park and our arena is the Consol Energy Center. All three are newer venues that offer great amenities, food, seating, and arguably (but in my mind, unquestionably) feature the best professional sporting teams around.

Heinz Field

Heinz Field is a newer and state of the art stadium where our PITTSBURGH Steelers ("Stillers") and the University of PITTSBURGH ("PITT") Panthers football teams play. It is an open stadium that can seat the large crowds in comfort. It is also a venue for some of PITTSBURGH's larger concerts.

When you attend a Steelers game in PITTSBURGH, you are taken back by this massive stadium that bleeds Black and Gold colors. The stadium is impressive but the energy

and passion for the Steelers is the thing that takes your breath away on game day.

To say that the PITTSBURGH fans are passionate is an enormous understatement. PITTSBURGH Steeler fans extend across the nation and are nothing short of fanatical about our team.

Approaching game day means a buzz in the city and on game day there is no denying the indescribable excitement. If there is one thing on your bucket list that you must check off; it is a Steelers game at Heinz field.

PNC Park

PNC Park is a beautiful baseball stadium that opens to downtown ("Dahn-tahn") PITTSBURGH ("Burgh"). Voted one of the nicest baseball Stadiums in the nation, this is a venue that will surely impress you.

The stadium doesn't go for mass but instead is a smaller, more intimate stadium that was designed for a cozier

field and a first rate experience. There really is not a bad seat in the park as you are always close to the action.

Another great benefit is the vast amounts of food options that you can indulge in. Not just hot dogs and chips; You can sample Primanti's, a dog with Pierogi's on it, and many more great items.

Watching the PITTSBURGH Pirates is always a nice fun activity but there are few greater ways to spend a summer evening than with the Pirates at PNC Park!

Consol Energy Center

The PITTSBURGH Penguins have always been a longstanding favorite of sports fans. With hockey superstars from past to present, we have always adored the PITTSBURGH Penguins.

The Consol Energy Center is the newest of the three sporting venues in PITTSBURGH (Finished in 2010) and is home of the great PITTSBURGH PENGUINS.

YINZER BIBLE

This arena features a modern design and is certainly considered one of the best hockey venues in the NHL.

The new stadium design is fan centric. This lends to great seating throughout the stadium and of course, amazing food.

If you are in-season, experiencing a Pen's game is absolutely fantastic. Unlike its counterparts, this is a closed ceiling stadium which means that the energy after the Pen's score is simply magnified!

It is comfortable and inspiring to say the very least. Even if you come from another city, you will find yourself hard pressed not to root for the Pen's in this amazing venue.

SOUTH SIDE

The South Side is a stretch of bars that is just over the bridge from downtown. It is a well-known "drinking hole" for the city where bars extend for miles down the main thoroughfare named East Carson Street.

This area of town also boasts some shops, restaurants, and many city homes. Some of these homes are located on the "Slopes" or extremely steep hills on the southern side of the area and offer nice views of the city in a very affordable location.

This is a region where you will find many college students celebrating every night of the week, as well as some locals watching the out of town games and yes, there is a Primanti's there too!

If you are visiting and like to partake in some Hops and Barley brew, you must visit the South Side and experience the bustling nightlife.

One great find is the Hofbräuhaus which is located at the Southside Works (*2705 South Water St., PITTSBURGH, PA 15203, Phone: (412) 224-2328*). Hofbräuhaus is a very fun establishment modeled after the legendary and historic Hofbräuhaus of Munich, Germany. It is the closest thing to being in Germany and is guaranteed to be a good time.

It is also conveniently located next to one of PITTSBURGH Cheesecake Factory Restaurants so you can grab a nice snack before and probably after.

COLLEGES AND UNIVERSITIES

PITTSBURGH is home to A LOT of students that help create a very vibrant city. This city of academia includes institutions such as Carnegie Mellon University, University of PITTSBURGH, Duquesne University, Carlow University, Robert Morris University, Point Park University, Chatham, and more. It kind of creates a college town inside of a bigger city, especially when you are near to the college campuses.

The credentials and reputation of each school vary but all have good standings in Western, PA. Carnegie Mellon of course is the most well known of the group and it carries its prestige across the nation and beyond.

The presence of these universities also means that there is no shortage of younger adults in the city, which creates a great amount of energy and enthusiasm around the area. Make no mistake about it, the restaurants and bars are forever grateful for the strong academia presence in PITTSBURGH.

Academia also means that you will encounter many PITTSBURGH residents that aren't originally from PITTSBURGH. Instead, these "Transplants" came to the PITTSBURGH area for school, fell in love with the city, and never left. Many of my friends in fact are from other cities but just adored PITTSBURGH and stayed.

VISITORS GUIDE

So what do you do if you are a tourist, new resident, or someone that doesn't get around much? The answer is, A LOT! PITTSBURGH is rich in culture, entertainment, dining, and so much more, which means that there is no shortage of activity for you. Just get out and start socializing as the PITTSBURGH population is very friendly. It is not at all unusual to find many people who are also visiting the cities and it is always fun to exchange great tips and trivia.

Being a PITTSBURGH native may mean that I am biased toward the city. However, I have heard countless tourist and new arrivals rave about the city for its culture, history, dining, and entertainment aspects. In fact,

YINZER BIBLE

PITTSBURGH is rapidly increasing in tourism from not only people that reside in other cities but also other countries. It has also been ranked as the most "Livable City" by a popular well-regarded publication.

I think that the thing that strikes people most about PITTSBURGH is its combination of beauty, food, culture, and entertainment. It has many great hotels, a state-of-the-art convention center. It is clean, safe, and relatively inexpensive. It is a good city to be a part of and is well-liked by those who visit (who often become frequent visitors).

So if you are from out of town and are planning a trip to PITTSBURGH or you are just looking for some things to do; below are some hard to beat suggestions that most people would agree upon.

A Priceless View

Take Advantage of the View: PITTSBURGH boasts some of the most breathtaking views of any major city. Those who know the city, know that it is best viewed from the top of Mt. Washington along Grandview Avenue. There are several overlook points that allow you to have magnificent views of the city where you can spend some time relaxing and enjoy the majestic beauty. It is also a great place for some great photo opportunities and/or selfies.

If you want to do so over a drink, head over to the Coal Hill Steakhouse at the Grandview Saloon (*1212 Grandview Avenue*). This establishment quite possibly has one of the best outdoor overlooks of the city that are available to its

patrons from the outside deck. It is a great choice for a drink and doesn't require a reservation.

Taking in the view while dining is also easily done. There are many restaurants to choose from but my favorite seafood restaurant is Monterey Bay Fish Grotto (*1411 Grandview Avenue, PITTSBURGH, PA 15211*). This is a restaurant that gets filled up quickly so phone ahead for a reservation *(412) 481-4414*. Or alternatively, you can grab a drink and snack at their bar that features the same stunning view as the restaurant.

Inclines:

Ride the Incline: While you are on Mt. Washington, take the Monongahela Incline (one of two inclines in the city) down Mt. Washington and into Station Square.

The inclines offer some of the greatest views in PITTSBURGH and provide iconic history as you descend over its tracks.

Station Square:

Station Square is a great place to grab a bite or drink at one of the many bars and restaurants. It offers a very beautiful and unique perspective of the city from just across the river of central downtown.

One of the greatest and most distinctive restaurants in the Station Square area is the Grand Concourse (*100 W Station Square Dr, PITTSBURGH, PA 15219 (412) 261-1717*) which is an upscale restaurant specializing in Seafood. It resides in an old train station with character that cannot be matched.

A meal that will also go unmatched is the extraordinary Sunday brunch buffet (a reservation is recommended). It is a buffet like I have never experienced anywhere else and it expands over three rooms typically with relaxing piano music to accompany your meal.

As a converted majestic train station, this restaurant is known to be one of the best in the city and I wholeheartedly agree.

Also in Station Square is the home base of the *Just Ducky Tours* (412-402-3825). These amphibious vehicles take you on a tour of the city and then like a duck, drive you right into the river for a nice boat ride before returning to the Station Square nest. It is a very informative tour that provides distinctive views and many interesting points of interest.

YINZER BIBLE

Even a native can learn much from this tour. Having lived in PITTSBURGH all my life, I was shocked by how much I learned on this unusual tour and I love taking my out of town visitors on this nicely guided experience.

A very fun way of seeing PITTSBURGH is by Segway. Guided tours are offered by a company called Segway in Paradise (*100 West Station Square Drive, PITTSBURGH, Pennsylvania 15219, (412) 412-337-3941*).

The tours are usually two hours and give you a perspective that is very unique. It comes highly recommended from those visiting and our residents.

Seasonal Ice Skating is a daily activity at PPG place in the wintertime. This outdoor skating rink centers around a large Christmas tree while wonderful holiday music accompanies your fun. The unique mirrored PPG buildings engulf the rink for a very magical experience.

In the warmer weather, this same area is transformed into a stunningly beautiful fountain that comes alive with powerful synchronized water jets. Many children bring their swimming suits and splash in the puddles as the beautiful fountain jets around them create numerous formations of vertical water.

Market Square:

Just through the building from the PPG rink or fountain (depending on the time of year), is a charming little square called Market Square. This square is in the center of the city and features many shops and restaurants. During the weekdays, the square is a lunchtime gathering place for those that work downtown as well as many tourists.

This area is also a venue for concerts in the summer and the center point for the outdoor St. Patrick's Day events in March.

There are many tables where you can enjoy some food, and yes, there is a Primanti's here too! A great find in Market Square is the Original Oyster House (*20 Market Square, PITTSBURGH, PA 15222)* which is PITTSBURGH's oldest bar

and restaurant (established in 1870). It is an intimate historic landmark that serves great seafood.

Naturally they do Oysters very well but your will find many other things on their menu to tantalize your taste buds.

Casino:

You wouldn't know it from the bland exterior styling, but PITTSBURGH is home to a casino called the Rivers Casino *(777 Casino Drive, PITTSBURGH, PA (412) 231-7777)*.

It is located just minutes from the city near our more aesthetically attractive Science Center and a stones throw from the Steelers stadium.

The Casino is very popular among the many tourist who visit the city each year. It is a modern attraction with excellent parking, lots of excitement, and is centrally located.

Science Center:

The Carnegie Science Center (*One Allegheny Avenue, PITTSBURGH, PA 15212, Phone: 412-237-3400*) is a venue that features many interactive activities for people of all ages. The amazing Omnimax Theatre features a screen that surrounds the room and a state of the art sound system to put you in the film. The center also has a retired submarine, aquariums, laser shows, large train village, and many kids programs.

It is a great experience although tends to be a bit pricey for a simple stop in.

Phipps Conservatory:

Phipps Conservatory and Botanical Gardens in Oakland (*1 Schenley Park, PITTSBURGH, Phone: (412) 622-*

6914), is a wonderful place to peruse some breathtaking greenhouses that house plants from all over the world. It is a lovely way to spend an afternoon as you maze through seasonal gardens and decorations.

It is a place of relaxation that can simply dissolve stress as you meander through many differently themed rooms. It is a sanctuary of sorts with smells and sites that will leave you with a more relaxed state of mind (especially in the cold months).

Shenley Park

Neighboring Phipps is Shenley Park. Shenley Park is a good place to take a outdoor walk while overlooking the modern looking and world renowned Carnegie Mellon University.

Besides bordering Carnegie Mellon (CMU) and the University of PITTSBURGH, there are great walking trails and even a golf course.

On certain nights in the summertime, there are outdoor movies on Flagstaff Hill (central Schenley Park) that begin just after dusk. Bring a blanket and a snack and enjoy a nice outdoor movie at no cost.

Shadyside

Just a mile away is Shadyside that features upscale shopping on Walnut Street. If you are looking for a restaurant while shopping, you can grab a bite at Pamela's restaurant or the always delicious China Palace. If you are looking for a little more trendy food, Casbah (*229 S Highland Ave,*

PITTSBURGH, Phone: (412) 661-5656) can be found on the other end of Shadyside on South Highland Avenue.

A great dessert can be found just steps away at the legendary Prantl's Bakery on Walnut Street.

Many restaurants and bars adorn the streets of Shadyside and so just walking the main thoroughfares of

South Highland, Walnut Street, and Ellsworth will provide you with a host of options.

As we mentioned, you really can't experience PITTSBURGH without taking in a game. So depending on the season, grab tickets as it is a great way of experiencing the culture and a way to rub elbows with our beloved Yinzers. Whether it is hockey, football, or baseball, it is hard to be a part of PITTSBURGH without enjoying a sporting event.

Kennywood

PITTSBURGH has a great amusement park called Kennywood (*4800 Kennywood Blvd., West Mifflin, PA 15122, PHONE: 412.461.0500*). Just 15 minutes from the city, Kennywood boasts great roller coasters, modern (and terrifying) thrill rides, and some of the best french fries in the

city (found at the Potato Patch in Kennywood). It is a park that combines history and modern thrills that has been a part of PITTSBURGH since 1898.

It is a park for all ages (and stomachs) so don't be hesitant to experience Kennywood!

PITTSBURGH Zoo & PPG Aquarium

The PITTSBURGH Zoo & PPG Aquarium (*One Wild Place, PITTSBURGH, PA 15206, Phone: (412) 665-3640*) is also in the Kennywood area if you feel adventurous. Spanning over 77 acres with approximately 90 primate animals, there is a lot to see all year round.

The zoo cares for over 20 endangered species and is only one of six major zoo and aquarium combination. The

aquarium features 4,000 exotic fish featuring a stingray tunnel and two story open fish habitat.

The zoo does a wonderful job of presenting the habitats close enough to the visitor trails. It is a wonderful zoo that is hard to beat.

Gateway Clipper

The Gateway Clipper Fleet (412-355-7980) is a group of small ships that vary in size and style that cruise the PITTSBURGH rivers. You can catch a ride on one of these vessels from Station Square and enjoy many unique perspectives of the city.

These boats are available for charter for an entire group or you can join a general public guided ride. The rides are usually an hour to two and they will unquestionably unveil

the city to you in a way that you have never seen before. Many of the tours are guided with some great facts about the city.

As a note, these boats are not known for their food so you would be well advised to eat at the restaurants in Station Square prior to climbing onboard.

FESTIVALS AND BIG ATTRACTIONS:

Festivals and Big Attractions: PITTSBURGH has many great festivals throughout the year that are a lot of fun and can really help you experience the culture and people. If you time your time with one of them, you can maximize your experience.

St. Patrick's Day Festival

PITTSBURGH is not known to be a purely Irish city but you wouldn't know it on St. Patrick's Day. Head to Market Square with a warm coat and hat for some music, fun, and a

lot of beer. This is a day where you will definitely want a cab handy or perhaps a room to nap in the downtown area so book your hotel early. This festival is a lot of fun and is always a "*somewhat*" memorable experience for those that like to celebrate the day in style.

Regatta

In the summer, we have the PITTSBURGH Regatta which features speed boats, air shows, and much more. It is held right at the point in downtown and is a great way to enjoy a summer weekend.

In addition to many great food tents from around the city, the Fourth of July Fireworks usually coincide with this event that provides a double band for the buck.

The summer regatta is a long standing tradition that wraps around the downtown area and is always full of activities and excitement at our Point.

The PITTSBURGH Vintage Grand Prix

Schenley Park is the location of the famous PITTSBURGH Vintage Grand Prix that takes place in July. This event is America's largest vintage race and also the only one of its kind to run on city streets.

150 cars will race through the 450 acre park and golf course and will draw nearly 200,000 spectators.

In addition to the races; car owners from across the nation show their cars in their brand category across the park. You will find everything to vintage Ford's to new McLaren's and everything in-between.

There is food, music, and so many great people that share the passion and history for automobiles. If you are interested in cars, THIS is a great event to attend (Note: from someone else who immensely enjoys cars).

Fourth of July

If you have never experienced PITTSBURGH fireworks, it an absolute must see. I have been a fan of fireworks since I was a child but PITTSBURGH offers such a unique venue for fireworks.

The first thing that you will notice is that the PITTSBURGH geography puts our fireworks into a natural stadium of sorts. With natural bleachers on either side of the city, you have the perfect venue for watching the fireworks.

The firework displays in PITTSBURGH are some of the most unforgettable displays in the country. The always enormous and perfectly synchronized displays cast beautiful colors on the rivers as the booms echo through the valley.

This display, held at the "Point" right in the middle of the city, will unquestionably give you chills as it lights up the night. It is something that can be enjoyed year after year with a different perspective every time depending on your viewing location (Mt. Washington, Point State Park, Stadium, South Side, restaurants, hotels, etc.). It is an amazing summer tradition.

PITTSBURGH Air Show

Every summer there is an air show held in the greater PITTSBURGH area. Depending on the year, it may be held at

a local Air Force Base near the PITTSBURGH International Airport or perhaps the Latrobe Airport about an hour outside of PITTSBURGH.

This air show has many of the most impressive military aircraft on display as well as many civilian and vintage aircraft. Many aerial demonstrations take place including an occasional visit from the Blue Angels or other synchronized flying team.

There are always many modern and historical airplanes on display as well as our Men and Women in the Armed Services. If you have never been in close proximately to one of America's brilliant fight jets, you will be left in awe.

Fall Festivals:

Fall is one of my favorite times in PITTSBURGH. The comfortable weather in October along with the beautiful autumn foliage make it an ideal time to enjoy the town. PITTSBURGH boasts several wonderful fall festivals that can be found at various places throughout the city and region. Two of my favorites are the one held at Sorgels and the one held at Trax Farms. Sorgels (located in the North Hills at *2573 Brandt School Rd, Wexford, PA 15090*) and Trax Farms (located in the South Hills at 528 Trax Road, Finleyville, PA 15332) are working farms that also have wonderful gift shops, baked goods, and of course fresh produce year round.

In the fall, they morph into a destination for many PITTSBURGHERS where you can go on a tractor ride, enjoy a corn maize, feed farm animals, find a pumpkin, and so much

more. The festive environment is intoxicating and it is a great place to spend an afternoon with your significant other, friends, or family.

It is a great place to simply enjoy the fall weather in a natural setting.

Renaissance Festival:

The PITTSBURGH Renaissance Festival (located at *112 Renaissance Lane, West Newton, PA 15089, Phone: (724) 872-1670*) is an annual event that boasts all of the glory of the Renaissance times including some amazing costumes.

Those that have participated in these festivals know that they need no introduction whatsoever. It is fun festival that is fun for enthusiasts as well as any tourists and/or family. And yes, turkey legs are there for the enjoyment!

Three Rivers Arts Festival:

The Three Rivers Arts Festival is held once a year in the early summer (typically June or July) in downtown PITTSBURGH. It generally spans a week and is a great place where you can view and purchase art, sample some great food, and take in the city. There are artist from both far away and locally and feature very unique paintings and sculptures.

It is hard to visit and not find at least something that ends up in your residence but even if you purchase nothing, the experience is fantastic.

Shadyside Arts Festival:

The Shadyside Arts Festival is held in the center of Shadyside on Walnut Street. Like the Three Rivers Arts Festival, you can peruse many tents with inexpensive to very

expensive local art. With approximately 150 artists, this is a great place to enjoy the PITTSBURGH culture (typically held in late August).

Holiday Shopping and Activities

PITTSBURGH is an absolute gem during the holidays. The holiday spirit can be felt from everyone you meet and everywhere you go as the city sparkles with holiday lights. Planning the perfect holiday weekend might include looking at the large nativity scene at the UPMC / US Steel Building on Grant street, gazing at the magnificent Christmas tree at the PGH Courthouse Building and then taking a walk down to enjoy the ice skating rink and holiday displays in PPG square.

If you are in the mood for shopping, you have an enormous Macy's department store downtown right at your fingertips, local boutiques, and many other downtown shops.

If you want to enjoy wonderful displays of Christmas lights, there are two great options. Just 25 minutes outside of the city is the Celebration of Lights at Hartwood Acres. If you feel a little more adventurous, an absolutely spectacular display of lights is just a slightly farther drive (50 minutes) at Oglebay Resort and Conference Center (*465 Lodge Drive, Wheeling, WV 26003, (304) 243-4000*).

This Festival of Lights is in nearby Wheeling, WV and is a popular destination for many PITTSBURGH residents. The lights are absolutely breathtaking and will unquestionably put you in the holiday mood. While you are there, it is a good place to also grab dinner at the Wilson Lodge dining room or

Glassworks restaurant. Or you can even pamper yourself at their first class spa.

PITTSBURGH and the surrounding areas take holiday decorations very seriously and lights can be seen on almost every residence, restaurant, and shop.

WHAT WE DRINK

PITTSBURGH is not a martini town (although we have our martini bars) but instead more of a beer town. And when PITTSBURGH reaches for a beer, they favor the "Iron". Iron City has been the preferred beer in PITTSBURGH for decades as it was founded and locally brewed on Liberty Avenue for years (adjacent to the famous JNR I, II, III Riley Distribution Company).

Although the brewery recently left its post on Liberty Avenue and moved out of the (city to Latrobe, PA), the beer still remains a strong choice among the Yinzer/PITTSBURGH population. Whether it is a cold Iron at a Pirates or Pens

game, or one at one of the local bars, it is a beer that flows through the veins of PITTSBURGHERS and helps complete the Yinzer experience.

Holding an Iron doesn't make you a PITTSBURGHER as an out of towner but it does lend you some credibility as it indicates good taste on your part and an interest of taking part in our local culture.

WHERE WE DRINK

Where we grab a drink is just as diverse as the people in PITTSBURGH. There are many neighborhood bars in PITTSBURGH where you can connect with friends or make new ones. From little dive bars to large clubs, there is no shortage of watering holes in PITTSBURGH.

I think that every one has such interesting people, experiences, and stories that you will be hard pressed to find just one.

However, the heart of the bar scene is unquestionably the South Side. With block after block of bars, there is

absolutely no shortage of spots where you can enjoy your beer of choice.

Some of the classic bars are Mario's, Smokin' Joes, Jacks, and Margaretville. While these are long standing institutions, there are so many more good places but these are bars that have stood the test of time and are always a favorite of the PITTSBURGH crowd.

HOW WE LIVE

PITTSBURGH is probably one of the friendliest mid sized cities in the country.   People are very warm and maintain a sense of small town friendliness. We rally around the sports, food, music, and more as you have found from reading. You will experience a unique camaraderie in the city and find that PITTSBURGH is kind of like one big quirky family.

Without really experiencing it, it is very hard to understand. PITTSBURGH is clearly a work hard, play hard kind of a city. Thus, you can find a lot of great happy hours,

dance clubs, or social events that allow us to burn off the steam from a long day of hard work.

Another thing about the city is that the people are very real. It is not a pretentious city where everyone is trying to look or act famous. It is a place where generally speaking, what you see, is what you get.

It is this sort of attitude that makes PITTSBURGH such a great city to live and/or visit.

GETTING AROUND

If you haven't grown up in PITTSBURGH, getting around the city is more like a stroke of luck than an intentional plan (at least at first). PITTSBURGH is divided by three rivers called the Monongahela (or "Mon"), Ohio, and Allegheny rivers. The rivers shape the city into a tight and somewhat confusing triangle as opposed to the grid pattern of a Midwest type city.

The unusual shape means that the city is not the traditional square blocks of other cities and this is where the confusion is routed. In addition, streets go many different

ways and you can easily find yourself in a restricted lane or facing the wrong way on one of the many one-way streets.

In addition to the lack of directional intuitiveness, PITTSBURGH is known as the "City of Bridges." Many of the bridges and ramps snake through the area. Getting on the wrong one can take you on a ten minute forced sightseeing trip.

Traffic is also something that PITTSBURGHERS are used to. As you approach any of the tunnels, you will find the best "Lane Jockeying" North of the Meadows horse track.

When it comes to driving in snow, PITTSBURGHERS are masters. There are few cities on earth where you have to face off with an icy cliff every winter morning. There are many slopes, hills, and cliffs in PITTSBURGH and we are pretty

good at navigating them in all conditions. Cobblestones are not easy to drive on when icy but we seem to have a knack for it. After all, nothing is going to stop us from getting to Primanti's or a Steelers game.

There are also bridges that merge major artieries together, infuse downtown traffic, and end in a tunnel just 300 ft away with one exit in-between. Yes, this is PITTSBURGH traffic!

From a transportation perspective, PITTSBURGH cabs are pretty common in the downtown area (especially near the hotels and convention center) but become less common in other areas of the city unless called for.

YINZER BIBLE

As long as you avoid rush hour traffic, you can take your time but avoid looking in the rear-view mirror as many PITTSBURGHers are eager to get to their destinations.

TRANSPORTATION

PITTSBURGH doesn't boast the major public transportation systems of a New York or Chicago. It is a walking city where you can get many places by foot or bike. However, many things are spread out far enough that visitors will choose to rent a car.

A cab service like Yellow Cab (412) 321-8100 is always nice for the locals and visitors when the night gets a little wild.

Flying in and out of the city is quite easy. The airport is only about 30 minutes (without traffic) outside of the city and flights are regular. Like all major airports, a host of car rental companies are stationed at the airport.

YINZER BIBLE

The PITTSBURGH underground service or subway service is called the "T". In 2012 a new route to the stadiums and casino was sanctioned to allow easier access to the sporting venues (No surprise in PITTSBURGH). It is an underground train until it reaches the other edge of the city where it surfaces to cross over to Station Square and then to the South Hills.

It is an adequate system for many people although if you are just moving from point to point within downtown, it is typically faster to walk.

There is also an extensive bus system that reaches every direction of PITTSBURGH. These buses called PAT buses (Port Authority Transportation) are a major thoroughfare for those in the city and surrounding areas.

HISTORY OF PITTSBURGHERS

Many people often ask the origins of PITTSBURGH. "So when did PITTSBURGH begin???" Settlers arrived in PITTSBURGH in the 1700's. It is a unique geography that was comprised of the major highway systems of the time that in those days were called the rivers. This made it a great place for colonization and growth.

Over the years PITTSBURGH evolved and discovered that strategic mineral deposits and excellent river access helped the city thrive in one of its best known commodities; steel. With so many steel mills in operation during the 1800 and 1900's, it was no surprise that this steel mecca became

known as the Steel City and was full of proud blue collar workers along with a growing population of white collar.

We thank our forefathers who helped build this city into what is today. It is truly an evolution that has spanned over hundreds of years and will continue evolving as time passes.

In fact, the new boom in PITTSBURGH is the natural gas business. With an enormous influx of energy companies and personnel, we see a new chapter in PITTSBURGH growth.

TOPOGRAPHY:

The topography is one of the most unique parts of PITTSBURGH architecture. Over millions of years, the Monongahela and the Allegheny rivers, which join to meet the Ohio, have carved through the landscape to form the many crevices and hilltops that make our city so unique. And the heart of our beautiful city sits at the very point where these rivers meet.

With a landscape such as this, we should not be surprised by the number of bridges and tunnels. The number of bridges that expand the greater PITTSBURGH area is

estimated to be around 1,800 with about a quarter of them being in the City of PITTSBURGH.

PITTSBURGH is always described as being "Hilly and windy" and not to mention beautiful. We have a very unique topography that is different from anywhere else you may have visited.

ARCHITECTURE

Just as unique as the culture, food, and people in PITTSBURGH is the wonderful architecture. Whether you have lived in PITTSBURGH all of your life or are just there for the day, there is no arguing that PITTSBURGH is one of the most architecturally unique cities in the eastern U.S. Take a walk downtown and look up at the various buildings that make up the skyline. You will be awestruck by the amount of character and detail in many of the buildings.

You have so much to admire; From the ultra post modern PPG building, to the classic styles of decades past (Omni Penn), to gothic churches and buildings.

Shown: PPG Building Complex

One must see is the beautiful mirrored building complex of PPG in the heart of downtown PITTSBURGH. Constructed in the early 1980's, it's 20,000 pieces of mirrored glass are a beautiful sight and home to many offices.

The highest of the PPG complexes is PPG One that spans 40 stories into the PITTSBURGH skyline. With floor to ceiling windows, those that work in this complex are truly fortunate.

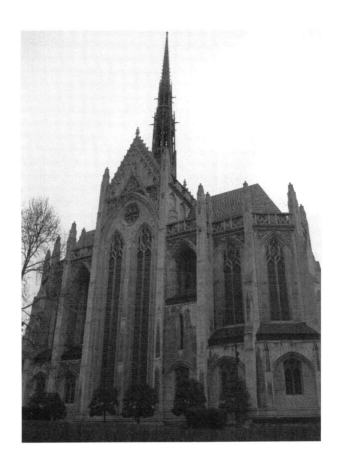

Heinz Memorial Chapel

The Heinz Memorial Chapel in Oakland is a place
where people worship and celebrate life's graces. It was

constructed in the 1930's and is crafted of limestone and solid oak with astounding vaulted ceilings and marvelous stained glass.

The chapel was a gift of German-American Henry John Heinz, founder of the H.J. Heinz Company, who wanted to honor his mother, Anna Margaretta Heinz, with a building at the university. Upon his death in 1919, Heinz's three surviving children (Howard, Irene, and Clifford) added to his bequest in order to memorialize their grandmother and honor their father. Their choice of a chapel for a memorial was guided by the concepts of education and religion which Anna Margaretta Heinz imbued in her children.

Howard Heinz, Chancellor John Gabbert Bowman, and Joh Weber, business manager and university secretary, were the driving energy behind the chapel's concept and execution.

Working with them were other members of the Heinz family, and two well-known clergymen, Dr. Hugh Thomson Kerr, pastor of Shadyside Presbyterian Church, and Dr. Henry Sloane Coffin, president of Union Theological Seminary.

Ground was broken in 1933 and the cornerstone laid in 1934. At the chapel's dedication on November 20, 1938 Howard Heinz spoke of the meaning of the memorial chapel:

"It is located in a community where my father was born and lived his life. It is on the campus of a university. As part of that university, it is dedicated to culture, and understanding response to beauty, and religious worship."

Chancellor Bowman commented at the cornerstone laying:

"The chapel is designed as a fitting center of worship which in various ways will rise at the University. The character, intensity, the level of that worship may change from generation to generation. The spiritual tide in men rises and falls. Through these changes though, the Chapel will stand, calm and undisturbed."

This special venue is home to countless wedding ceremonies. It is absolutely beautiful on the inside and out and is one of Oakland's and Pitt's most notable treasures.

Saint Paul's Cathedral

Saint Paul's Cathedral opened in 1906 in the Oakland

section of PITTSBURGH. This 247 foot structure is a

marvelous church that reflects the gothic style of the 14th Century.

SUMMARY

PITTSBURGH is an amazing city that boasts some of the greatest history, culture, food, people, and entertainment. All of this is what makes the BURGH the greatest city in the world and a place where it is good to be a part of!!!

Let your eyes be your guide and enjoy all that PITTSBURGH has to offer. After all, there is no better way to experience PITTSBURGH than to simply experience PITTSBURGH. Visit the places you enjoy and Yinz have fun living PITTSBURGH N'at.

- Yinzer Bible

Facebook: *Yinzer Bible*

YINZER BIBLE

Please feel free to join my Yinzer Bible Facebook page!!!! I welcome my new and old friends and enjoy our community together!

Made in the USA
San Bernardino, CA
07 December 2014